Micro and Small Enterprises for Sustainable Urban Livelihood

Micro and Small Enterprises for Sustainable Urban Livelihood

Dr. Karanam Viswa Bhushan

KALPAZ

First Published, 2021

Published by

Kalpaz Publications
C-30, Satyawati Nagar,
Delhi - 110052
Ph.: 011-47034999, 9811692060
www.kalpazpublications.com
E-mail: kalpaz@hotmail.com

Printed at: Gyan Press, Delhi.

Cataloging in Publication Data—DK
Courtesy: D.K. Agencies (P) Ltd. <docinfo@dkagencies.com>

Bhushan, Karanam Viswa, 1963- **author.**
Micro and small enterprises for sustainable urban livelihood / Dr. Karanam Viswa Bhushan.
pages cm
Includes bibliographical references.
ISBN 9789353246105 (HB)

1. Small business—Government policy—Ethiopia. 2. Poverty—Ethiopia—Prevention. 3. Rural development—Ethiopia. I. Title.

LCC HD2346.E8B48 2021 | DDC 338.6420963 23

Contents

Acknowledgements

First of all, I would like to thank the Almighty God for all his heavenly blessings.

I am grateful to my student Tewodros Tadesse who involved in the research work and participated sincerely throughout the work.

I thank all my colleagues for their sustained constructive and empowering comments, suggestions, which helped me to complete the task.

I extend my gratitude to my academic friends who encouraged for book publication

I would like to express my gratitude to my friend Christine Vinkx for her moral support and encouragement.

List of Tables

List of Figures

Chapter One

Introduction

In overall economic development, a micro and small enterprise was play a vital role in employment creation, income distribution, poverty reduction and local economic growth in developing world. It also had been significant contribution by creating better access to livelihood asset; empowering social, financial, physical, human and natural asset. This chapter presents the research problem and its approach; from which mainly consists of background of the study, statement of the problem, objective of the study, significant of the study, scope of the study, limitation of the study, definition of terms, and organization of the study.

1.1 Background of the Study

Various studies showed that persistence of poverty and unprecedented level of unemployment is characteristics of Ethiopia in general and urban areas in particular. Poverty in Ethiopia is a widespread phenomenon due partly to lack of economic opportunities and inadequate basic household income. Various suggestions were given by different scholars for addressing the persistent unemployment and poverty problems. Amongst, it is often argued that Micro and Small Enterprises (MSEs) play key roles in creating employment opportunities and generation of income. Scholars (e.g. Lukács, 2005; Olomi, 2006 and Geleta, 2013) confirmed the crucial role of MSEs in employment creation and poverty reduction. MSEs are important vehicle for addressing the challenges of unemployment, poverty and economic growth. They provide means of living to a large proportion of the population (Berhanu, 2005; Lukács, 2005). According to Olomi (2006), MSEs are major drivers of growth and development because they are labor intensive that are suitable for low skill wage laborer. Thus, they are means to absorb the cheaply available labor force, making them preferable than big industries (Ageba and Amha 2004; Amha and Ageba 2006; Olomi 2006).

The Ethiopian government has recognized the significance of MSEs and has given due attention to the area (Geleta, 2013). Ethiopia's industrial development strategy issued in 2003 also singled out the promotion of MSE development as one of the important instruments to create productive and dynamic private sector. The promotion of MSEs is justified on the grounds of enhancing growth with equity, creating long-term jobs, providing the basis for medium and large enterprise and promoting exports. In Ethiopia, establishing and being engaged in MSEs has become one of the livelihood activities pursued by many Ethiopian poor (Bekele and Muchie, 2009; Garoma, 2012).

Despite the recognition of the importance of MSEs, case specific study results been inadequate and lacking in the country every aspects in Addis Ababa in general and Gullele sub city in particular. Previous studies on MSEs used aggregated data at city and/or at sub city levels in considering its broader approach rather than giving attention for livelihood change the program brought at household levels.

These calls for more understandings of the role of micro and small enterprises for sustainable urban livelihood: the case of Gullele sub city; which need to be greatly improved through undertaking rigors research. In order to understand its impacts on household in reducing poverty, it may require conducting studies that explicitly reveal the effects of the program and major factors affect it. Therefore, this study will be aimed to investigate the role of micro and small enterprises for sustainable urban livelihood by considering Gullele sub city as case study.

1.2 Statement of the Problem

Currently, MSEs considered as among the crucial strategies to break out of poverty and develop sustainable livelihoods. Since, sustainable livelihoods can be a means of making the connect between our day-to-day lives and the means by which we can sustain all this into the future without damaging anyone else's prospects along the way; it has significant impacts in empowering households access to labor, employment and assets (Stephen, 2013). Livelihood and income generation activities especially in urban areas like the city of Addis Ababa are closely linked with both availability of productive resources and the ability to use them sustainably and economically so as to improve the quality of residents in city. As a reason, it requires to make it socially sustainable particularly in urban areas when it can cope with and recover from stresses and shocks, and maintain or enhance its capabilities and assets, both now and in the future, while not undermining the natural resource base (Kabiret .al, 2012).

In consequence, giving adequate recognition for the micro and small enterprise development has paramount importance to bring countries economic development to lift countries out of poverty (Wolfenson, 2001). It also plays as are driving force for economic growth, job creation, and poverty reduction and as feeder service to large-scale industries (Fabayo, 2009).

In light of this, Micro and Small Enterprise Development Program in Ethiopia has been given due attention by government since 2004/2005. However even if the government of Ethiopia has taken various measures to make the overall environment suitable including the city of Addis particularly for youth and women operators, the majority involved in the MSEs faced different obstacles related to capital, technical and managerial know-how, and access to credit, markets, raw materials and government support services (Mulu, 2007).

Given the importance and potential impact of the sectors on the overall development of the country and even in creating sustainable household livelihoods; undertaking different research like the present one have importance in closing the knowledge gaps and to see the effects of MSEs in supporting households livelihoods. Thus, the current study tries to examine the role of micro and small enterprises in realizing sustainable urban livelihood by considering Gulele sub city as case study.

1.3 Objective of the Study

1.3.1 General Objectives

The general objective of the study is to investigate the role of micro and small enterprises in realizing sustainable urban livelihood by considering Gulele sub city as case study.

1.3.2 Specific Objectives

The specific objective of the studies

1. To assess the contribution of MSEs on urban livelihood assets of the households;
2. To examine the effects of MSEs in developing urban households wellbeing/ wealth status;

3. To explore the livelihood strategies used by MSEs to cope up various challenges and problems found in the sectors.

1.4 Research Questions

This research will attempt to answer the following questions:

1. What is the contribution of MSEs in creating better access to various urban livelihood assets for selected households?
2. How organizing in MSEs empowering urban households wellbeing/ wealth status?
3. What livelihood strategies used by MSEs to cope up with various challenges and problems found in the sectors?

1.5 Significances of the Study

Previously, very few studies were undertaken to show the contribution and the effects of MSEs in bringing sustainable urban livelihoods. Few studies existing in this regard lack integration and consistency with the issue of linking the role of MSEs in bringing households sustainable livelihoods. Hence, the current study has the importance of:

- adding knowledge on the gap created around the issues;
- Exploring the contribution of MSEs in creating better access to the different livelihood assets for operators and urban households?
- Investigating the role of MSEs in empowering urban households wellbeing/ wealth status?
- Assessing livelihood strategies used by MSEs to cope up with various challenges and problems found in the sectors?

- Provide policy makers, researchers, institutions, Addis Ababa City Administration, Gulele Sub City etc. with adequate, sufficient and reliable data so as to improve the contribution of the MSEs for sustainable urban livelihoods and development endeavors.

1.6 Delimitation of the Study Area

For the sake of making the research manageable, this study has limited in scope, time, and coverage areas. Accordingly, the study will be undertaken in Gullele Sub City Administration. Consequently, the analyses of the study will also restricted to the investigation of the contribution and the effects of MSEs in bringing sustainable urban livelihoods; for those only officially organized and have production areas.

1.7 Organization of the Study

The study has five chapters. The first chapter deals with an introductory part of the paper in which the background of the research briefly described and the problem to be researched is identified. Chapter two will be discussed about the theoretical foundation and gives a critical review of the various theories that have bearing on the problem, and a review empirical literature in which basic terms, relations and correlation of ideas related to the study has been conceptualized; and indicate what has already been done in the field of study, which have great contribution for confirmation of the study objectives. Chapter three will consists of research methodology employed, sample unit and sampling techniques, data sources, and data analysis strategies. Whereas, chapter four will be deals with data/result presentation; analysis and interpretation, while the last part, (chapter five) will presents summary of key findings, conclusion and recommendations of the study.

Chapter Two

Review of Related Literature

A literature review is a scholarly paper, which includes the current knowledge including substantive findings, as well as academic and methodological contribution to a particular topic. It is also review a secondary source and do not report new or original experiment work.(Wikipedia).

This chapter tries to review empirical and theoretical foundations related to the investigation of about the contribution of MSEs in creating better access to livelihood assets; empowering household's wealth status; and how we can assess livelihood strategies used by MSEs to cope up with livelihood shocks and crises. Moreover, the chapter highlight about the conceptual frame works developed by the researcher so as to give guidance for proper selection methodologies used and adequately answer the research question raised in chapter one.

2.1 Review of Empirical Studies

2.1.1 The role of SMEs in Economic Growth and Development

The growing interest in the advance of SMEs among developing nations is explained by their significant potential to generate income, sustainable livelihoods and to bring more about equitable social and economic development both in rural and urban areas (Small, 2004; Williams, 2006). In developing economies including Ethiopia, MSEs play a crucial role in employment creation, income distribution, poverty reduction, rural development and industrial development (Abor & Quartey, 2010). Accordingly, governments of these countries have been providing extensive support to their SME sectors through implementation of various programs including subsidized credit schemes.

MSEs play critical roles in ensuring income stability, employment generation and economic growth (Schmitz, 1995). Policymakers, academics and economists have generally agreed that enhancing MSEs and promoting entrepreneurship can be a viable strategy for promoting economic development (Kongolo, 2010). Historically MSEs had a significant impact on households' livelihoods and economic development of many countries around the world and have had a substantial contribution in the industrialization process (Kongolo, 2010). The experiences of countries around the world confirm that stable economic development cannot be attained without a major presence of the MSEs sector in their economies (Naudé & Krugell, 2002). Many countries around the world have been supporting their MSEs sector by developing such policies and regulations which can flourish their businesses as without any doubt it is the best way to achieve economic development (Yusuf, 2001). MSEs represent a significant segment of the economies of developed countries and are regarded as the engine of growth in developing countries (Phaho & Pouris, 2008).

MSEs contribute a vast proportion of businesses in developing countries and are considered to be contributing to the generation of economic growth (Peci et al., 2012). In our country also, Gebremariam et al (2004) recognize a positive correlation between MSEs and economic growth. Abrahams (2003) contends that a well-supported MSEs sector has the potential to contribute to economic development in the same capacity as large businesses. A well-developed MSEs sector signifies a flourishing and growing economy (Kongolo, 2010). Several studies have confirmed that MSEs are positively correlated with national economic growth factors including Gross Domestic Product (GDP) (Newberry, 2006).

Significant variations exist in the size and economic activity of MSEs across countries and their contributions to economic growth varies accordingly. Since the Global Financial Crisis of 2008-2009, the interest in the role of MSEs in job creation and economic growth has significantly increased. The World Bank has estimated that 13 percent of GDP in developed countries and 3 percent of GDP in developing countries are constituted by MSEs loans whereas in OECD countries MSEs employ two-thirds of the total work force (Ardic et al., 2011).

There is a consensus in much of the literature reviewed for this study, that MSEs bring numerous benefits to the economies of both industrialized and developing countries (Advani, 1997). They increase employment, promote private ownership and entrepreneurship, enhance the skills and technical knowledge of the people, broaden the extent of new resource usage in the economy with more flexibility, intensify market competitions and enhance the export competitiveness of domestic economies. Other research findings also support the notion that MSEs play a major role in human resource development, contributing to tax and trade revenues, and boosting entrepreneurship in the society (Agyapong, 2010).

Academics argue that SMEs have numerous advantages over large scale businesses as they are more flexible and adaptable to new market conditions. Aggregate data suggests that SMEs demonstrate higher levels of growth than larger firms (Nichter & Goldmark, 2005). It has been suggested that the role of SMEs in economic growth and development can go beyond increasing per capita output and income as MSEs can bring about change in the structure of business and society (Hisrich et al., 2009).

For the reason many international organizations and donor countries share the view that MSEs promotion policies stimulate economic growth and aid in reducing high poverty rates in developing countries (Thornstenet al, 2004). The World Bank and the United Nations Industry and Development Organization (UNIDO) have been providing technical and financial assistance to developing countries through their private sector development programs. The World Bank supports MSEs development programs in developing countries based on the argument that MSEs generate incomes for the poor and thus constitute an effective poverty alleviation tool and sustainable livelihoods (Thorsten Beck et al., 2005).

Furthermore, it is widely recognized by policy makers and researchers that MSEs have enormous potential to create employment for the growing labor force (Kongolo, 2010). Employment generation is key to reducing the incidence of poverty and studies have found that private sector development, including the growth of MSEs, have the potential to create sustainable employment for the urban poor (Sokoto & Abdullahi, 2013). Mukras (2003) explains that the attraction of MSEs as an alternative generator of employment is due to their nature which is characterized by low start-up capital and low skill requirements.

2.1.2 Contribution of MSEs to Development of the Country

The rising level of poverty in developing countries poses a significant threat to the sustainability of these economies. The failure of countless development programs to impact the livelihoods of the poor has prompted a renewed focus on the role of MSEs as a way of attaining economic growth, sustainable livelihoods and development (Bowale & Akinlo, 2012).

MSE proponents argue that MSEs are an important mechanism for providing a variety of benefits in terms of socio-economic development (Advani, 1997). In many countries MSEs are considered as the engine of economic growth and development, generating employment and contributing to poverty reduction (Winfred, 2006). A well-developed MSEs sector is considered as one of the vital characteristics for a growing economy. MSEs constitute the vast majority of the enterprises in many developing countries and they play a significant role in their development (Kongolo, 2010). Empirical studies have found a positive role for MSEs on poverty alleviation efforts and empowering urban livelihoods (Mnenwa & Maliti, 2008). MSEs can support and sustain the livelihoods of urban households and their families, contributing to poverty alleviation (AKDN, 2008).

2.2 Definition and Enterprises Characterization in Ethiopia

Though Micro, Small and Medium Enterprises constitute the major share in terms of number in Ethiopia, there is no consistently placed definition for the sub sector by different bodies. In 1997, Ethiopia has defined Micro Enterprises as an enterprise with a total asset of less than 20,000 Birr ($1200) and Small Enterprises as Enterprises with a total asset of Birr 500,000 ($30,000) or less (FDRE, 1997). In this definition, the only base used is the total asset unlike international organizations' definition base (World BanK, 2015).To align the definition with at least some countries and international organizations, the country has revised the definition of Micro and Small Enterprises in 2011.

In the new definition, some of the attributes used by other countries and international organizations are addressed. In addition, the definition has segregated sectors as service and manufacturing. However, there is still confusion among different governmental organizations (e.g. Ministry of Trade, Central Statistics Agency, & Federal Micro and Small Enterprises Development Agency (FeMSEDA) in defining MSEs (Berihu, *etal*, 2014). Moreover, since it only focus on Micro and Small Enterprises, the new definition does not put any demarcation between Small and Medium; and Medium and large Enterprises. Central Statistics Agency (CSA) had grouped both large and Medium Enterprises together when these enterprises have employed more than 10 employees and used automated machinery. Though considering automation is advisable to categorize enterprises based on size (number of employees), automation of operations may help enterprises to reduce their employee. This argument weights much as blue-collar workers could be substituted by robots and other technological methods which may not necessarily enquire large number of employees as claimed by the CSA definition. Due to this gap, considering the CSA definition of Enterprises remains gloomy. Furthermore, IRACST – International Journal of Commerce, Business and Management (IJCBM), ISSN: 2319-2828 Vol. 6, No.1 Jan-Feb 2017 13 the definition of CSA does not consider the total asset; and service sectors are overlooked.

Federal Micro and Small Enterprises Development Agency (FeMSEDA), on the other hand, put definition of Micro and Small Scale Enterprises and categorize them from support provision perspective which contempt Medium Enterprises. With these precincts in defining and characterizing Micro, Small and Medium Enterprises in Ethiopia, adopting definition of MSMEs with slight modification is compulsory. To have uniform and consistent definition at least between different agencies and share similar concepts with international organizations and making accessibility of uniform data for the sector easy, adopting (G. Tom and V. Van der, 2008).

SMEs definition may be unwise since they discussed it as a single category without aligning it with Micro Enterprises. However, since there are international organizations that consider MSMEs, researchers believed that adapting international definition with slight modification considering the economic status of the country is logical? But the problem here is the development level of nations and asset requirement of enterprises within different industry makes comparison and adaptation of uniform definition difficult. Hence, to adjust with the economic status of the country, adjustment could be made by multiplying the total asset for the category by the GDP growth rate (IEG World Bank, 2013). Define Micro, Small and Medium Enterprises based on number of Employees, total asset and annual sales. As total asset and annual sales are similar in the definition set, taking total asset is chosen due to ease availability of data (Table 1).

Table 1: Define Micro, Small and Medium Enterprises based on number of Employees, total asset and annual sale

Enterprise indicators	*Number of employees*	*Total asset*	*Total annual sales*
Medium	>50; < 300	>$3,000,000;<$ 15,000,000	> $3,000,000; < $15,000,000
Small	>10; <50	>$100,000; < $3,000,000	> $100,000; < $3,000,000
Micro	<10	< $100,000	< $100,000

Source: Tom and Van der (2008).

When we compare the Ethiopian current definition of Micro and Small Enterprises with the above table, a very visible gap, resulted from the economic status of the country is observed. In Ethiopia, an enterprise is said to be micro, if it employees less than five employees and has a total asset of less than $6000 or Birr 100,000 for Manufacturing sector. When we compare it with the World Bank group number, it is approximately two times less for employees and its asset value is less by $94,000. When we do the same for Small Enterprises, the maximum number of employees is less than the World Bank's number by 20 and total asset is less than the same by $2,991,000 at the upper boundary limit. This figure is very significant that make comparison between Ethiopian Enterprises and Enterprises labelled by international organizations (e.g. World Bank) difficult.

To reduce the gap, forward move could be one solution for Ethiopia to increase the asset requirements of Enterprises i.e. as large number of enterprises are micro enterprises in Ethiopia (including retail stores), it is prudent to focus on relatively better sizes that could still be categorized under micro enterprises and leave out those enterprises with very low asset value as informal businesses except for registration purpose. Thus, the government can think of arranging micro enterprises based on their asset as Bottom- Micro, Middle Micro and Top Micro (BM-MM-TM) and adapt international definition of enterprises. Those Bottom and Middle Micro Enterprises could be considered as informal except for registration purpose. Enterprises to be taken as Top Micro will be those enterprises whose total asset value is not below 50% of the asset obtained from the product of GDP and World Bank Upper limit. For example, if an enterprise is with a total asset value of $5,500 where a country is with a GDP Growth rate of 11%, this value is a point where the top Micro starts as it is 50% of the to be upper limit ($11000/

2 = 5500) and hence, values more than or equal to this will be taken as Top Micro and values below this point constitutes Middle and bottom Micro with 50% intervals. Hence,$ 5,500 will be divided with two to set the point of demarcation between middle Micro and Bottom Micro. Accordingly, the values less than $2,750 is Bottom Micro and the value greater than or equal to $2750 and less than $5500 is Middle micro.

Consequently, enterprises with value less than $2,750 are Bottom, Enterprise with value of up to $ 5,500 is Middle and Enterprise above $ 5,500 is Top Micro. To obtain all these, the yearly GDP growth rate could be multiplied by the total asset establishment set by Word Bank (till it reaches exactly the same size of asset for each category) to drag the figure to the status and capacity of the country. For example, if the average GDP growth rate for a period is 11%, the total asset for Micro, Small and Medium Enterprises for the period will be as follows;

Table 2: Recommended Definition of MSMEs

Enterprise indicators	*Total asset*	*Total annual sales*
Micro Enterprises(Top)	>$5500TM ≤$11,000	≤$100,000
Small Enterprises	>$11,000;≤$330,000	>$100,000;≤$3,000,000
Medium Enterprises	>$330,000;≤$1,650,000	>$3,000,000;≤$15,000,000

Source: Own competition

As we are using GDP growth rate, the size and category of Enterprises may be fluctuated in different time period based on the GDP growth rate. And to avoid too much instability, it is advisable to set the criteria for enterprises category every five years when strategic plans are made. It is natural that a category frontier for enterprises may be changed if the GDP of the country is increasing or vice-versa as there is positive and strong relationship between SMEs and GDP per capita growth (Thorsten, 2005). But the average cumulative GDP growth rate is taken for range of periods more than a year. The above figure may seem difficult for some of the enterprises to reach at within less developed country like Ethiopia. However, unless the government can consider international basis of defining MSMEs, its march to the middle income level by 2015 may not be well supported from this sub sector. And hence, the government could make sure that funds from commercial banks and Micro Finance Institutions (MFI) are available for those enterprises beyond middle micro category so that the limited asset constraints will be solved. To make a smooth adjustment of the definition, certain assumptions are made to fulfill among others, as suggested by Amare (2017). These are:

- The country will have a positive growth in real GDP
- The world Bank definition of MSMEs as a base remain unchanged or if changed, the base will also be changed accordingly
- Enterprises size as Micro, Small and Medium is influenced by the country's real GDP
- Enterprises categorization limit (minimum and maximum) is revised based on the annual GDP growth rate

2.3 Ethiopian Micro and Small Enterprises Policy

In post 1991, unlike the predecessors regimes of Hailesellasie and the Derge, Ethiopia exercised decentralization policy and entered into the market economy. In addition, the country developed different policies towards poverty reduction. The Agriculture Development Led Industrialization (ADLI) was developed to increase the productivity of the agricultural sector and thereby forming both backward and forward linkages to the industrial sector. It was intended to achieve rapid growth in the agricultural sector and finally to promote and develop the manufacturing sector (MOI, 2006).

After ADLI, a Five-Year Development Strategy 2005/06 - 2009/10 named PASDEP developed, which was focusing mainly on poverty reduction both in rural and urban Ethiopia was developed. In this strategy, reducing the unemployment level and increasing the income of individual were the focus areas. Hence, as an instrument, MSEs were given great attention to achieve those objectives in urban Ethiopia (MOFED, 2006). As a result, different strategies were developed towards the promotion of MSEs. The 1997 Development strategy document and the report of industrial development strategy of Ethiopia were some of the outcomes of policies towards MSEs. In the document, great emphasis was given to MSEs and enabling institutional and policy environments were made easier and supportive to promote and expand the sector (*ibid.*).

Now a day in Ethiopia, according to MOTI (1997) report, great attention is given for the development of MSEs, as they are believed they can achieve rapid development through reducing unemployment and income inequalities and improving the living standards of the people at large. To achieve those objectives, target sub sectors are selected by the federal agency of Micro and Small Enterprises based on large market size, employment absorption capacity, short period of return over investment and the high role they play for poverty reduction. These sub-sectors include metal and woodwork, food processing, textiles and garment, construction materials production, municipal activities, Urban Agricultures and others. Hence, different stakeholders are also made to work in the promotion of MSEs and offices are allocated up to *weredas* levels to provide one-stop services to all the existing and emerging enterprises.

Moreover, according to national MSEs strategy, the Ethiopian MSEs sector is characterized by highly diversified activities, which can create job opportunities for substantial segment of the population. Accordingly, Ethiopia adopted its first MSEs Development strategy in 1997; the primary objective of the national strategy framework is to create an enabling environment for MSEs. Its specific objectives include facilitating economic growth and bring about equitable development, creating long-term jobs, strengthening cooperation between MSEs providing the basis for medium and large-scale enterprises; promoting exports, and balancing preferential treatment between MSEs and bigger enterprises. The intended MSEs, support include creating legal framework, improving access to finance, introducing different incentives schemes, encouraging partnerships, improving access to appropriate technology, information, advice and markets, and developing infrastructure (Gebrehiwot and Wolday, 2001 :6and 2004: 8).

The implementation of the strategy is planned to follow five stages. These are awareness creations, needs identification and implementation planning, resource identification, training of support agency staff and strengthening the business and entrepreneurial culture. The strategy indicated criteria for prioritizing MSEs for support. MSES which are based on local raw materials and labor intensive having greater inertia and inter-sectoral linkages (particularly with agriculture), import substitution and export capacity, MSEs engaged in activities that facilitate and promote tourism (MOTI, 1997)

In general, according to MOTI (1997) and MOI (2006), governmental bureaus, Micro Financing Institutions, Technical and Vocational Training Centers, productivity empowerment units, different NGOS, MSEs Councils, the project support units etc are made to work for the promotion of MSEs in Ethiopia. As a result, it is possible to understand from the above discussed policies that the current government is giving great attention for the sector to alleviate the abject poverty, unemployment and to achieve better income distributions.

2.4 Theoretical Foundation of Sustainable Livelihoods

The concept of sustainable livelihood proposes a more integrated and comprehensive approach. The sustainable livelihoods notion was first presented by the Brundtland Commission on Environment and Development in 1987. The 1992 United Nations Conference on Environment and Development extended the idea, supporting the attainment of sustainable livelihoods as an objective for poverty elimination (Iorio, 2010). Conway and Chambers (1992, p. 6) suggested the definition of a sustainable rural livelihood:

> *"A livelihood comprises the capabilities, assets (stores, resources, claims and access) and activities required for a means of living: a livelihood is sustainable which can cope with and recover from stress and shocks, maintain or enhance its capabilities and assets, and provide sustainable livelihood opportunities for the next generation; and which contributes net benefits to other livelihoods at the local and global levels and in the short and long term".*

This definition deals with the components that make up a livelihood, including assets such as financial resources, rights and claims, access to social networks and stores of food, as well as the activities in which an individual is engaged, and the range of capabilities they have that can contribute to living. It also, explains how this approach understands that livelihoods are sustainable when they are able to deal with the shocks and stresses and not only maintain these capabilities but also enhance the sustainability of them for the next generation (Birkmann, 2006). Meaning, if a livelihood is to be sustainable it can increase capabilities for long period of time (Carney, 2003).

2.4.1 Sustainable Livelihoods Approach

In the late 1980's the sustainable livelihoods approach term evolved in order to cater to the need to explore more effective methods of approaching poverty reduction (Scoones, 2009). Even though the sustainable livelihoods approach has been altered and refined for a broad array of resolutions, the primary notion of this approach has remained extraordinarily constant.

First, it is significant to understand that sustainable livelihoods approach was formulated from an approach to development of what can be called an 'intentional' approach. Chambers, a significant devotee of a sustainable livelihoods approach, claims that the way development specialists theorize poverty and development is actually dissimilar from how poor people themselves think about this Chambers (2011). Poor people observe poverty in a much more composite way than most development experts and they access a variety of approaches, not merely to make the most of income, but also to diminish the threat and to defend other things with meaning to them (social and cultural aspects).

The definition of sustainable livelihood by Chambers is closely allied with the assertion of Cowen and Shenton (1995), who advocate that development has numerous meanings, but the two basic forms of development are immanent development and the Intentional or interventionist development.

1. Immanent development is what people are doing anyway: this means a comprehensive procedure of

progression in human societies determined by an array of social and economic aspects together with developments in medicine, science, communication, the arts and governance etc. This is heightened by processes for instance globalization which facilitates the sharing of novel ideas and technologies.

2. Intentional (or Interventionist) development is a concentrated and fixed procedure in which non-government and government administrations initiate development programs and projects (often a series of correlated projects) to support the poor. The developments are typically bounded by time and resource, although they have an assumption that the improvements attained would endure after the particular project/development has ended.

Both forms – immanent development and intentional development – can and do take place in parallel. Typically, immanent development provides the broad context of change in cultures whereas 'Intentional' development happens as planned projects. Therefore, a country will be constantly undergoing 'Immanent' development as its private, public and "outsider" sectors progressively invest in infrastructure such as hospitals, roads, water provision, consumer products and services and education and training. The same country might also be host to a variety of development projects, possibly subsidized by foreign-based parties. Consequently, it is important to note the context created by immanent forms of development that can influence the form and outcomes of intentional development projects that seek to improve livelihoods.

2.4.2 Sustainable Livelihoods Framework

The sustainable livelihoods framework is one way of explaining the complex issues around poverty. It is not the only way, and it needs to be adapted, modified and made appropriate to local priorities and local circumstances (Coulthard et al., 2011). According to McGregor & Simon (2012) the Sustainable livelihoods framework is a tool frequently utilized by development bodies for formulating and evaluating development interventions. It emphasizes how individuals deliberately utilize the capitals accessible to them to forge livelihoods, and how development interventions can impact on obtainable capitals and integrate with them. Although it is usually the public face of the approach, the SLF does not or cannot aspire to capture all features of the sustainable livelihoods approach, and is one tool among a number that can be utilized when applying the approach.

The findings of the study conducted by Sallu (2010) reveal that there are a significant number of sustainable livelihoods frameworks that have been established and accepted by research organizations, NGOs and donor agencies. Out of many the most famous one is DFID's framework (Sallu 2010), though the key overall ideology applies to all. All of the frameworks emphasize the recipients of development projects as actors, who chose options, and make livelihoods grounded on the capitals accessible to them and the situation in which they exist. Intrinsically, these selections are grounded on apparent risks and opportunities. Dent (2013) reveals that one aspect of poverty is vulnerability to life's changes (the "vulnerability context") and can comprise exposure to aspects of changes for instance, shocks (war, drought, sickness or the death of a relative, etc.), seasonality (i.e. any changes related to the seasons such as commodity price fluctuations), and trends (inflation, decrease of certain types of employment, rising land prices, etc.).

2.4.3 DFID's Sustainable Livelihoods Framework

The notion of 'Sustainable Livelihoods' establish the

foundation of diverse 'Sustainable Livelihood Approaches' (SLA) and has been taken up by various development bodies, for example the British Department for International Development. The DFID has established a 'Sustainable Livelihood Framework' (SLF) that is one of the most extensively used livelihoods frameworks in development work. The Sustainable Livelihood Framework was incorporated in DFID's package for development collaboration in 1997 (Ferrol-Schulte 2013).DFID adapts the concept of Conway and Chambers' livelihoods, as consisting of assets, capabilities and activities which are needed for living (Bennett & Dearden, 2014). Adato and Meinzen-Dick (2002) shows how a livelihood can become sustainable if it can cope with shocks, and not just remain the same but also sustain and increase people's livelihood assets and capabilities both in their current condition and in the future. DFID maintains that there are numerous methods of implementing livelihoods methods and the implementation of the livelihoods method is adaptable and flexible to different local situations and it triggers a couple of essential ideologies.

Scoones (2009) illustrates that DFID has instituted a practice of adopting livelihoods approaches in program development and projects and in the evaluation and monitoring of existing activities. A key phase of this work is to recognize the importance of the existing livelihoods of the deprived people, specifically when steering livelihood investigations. According to Soltani (2012) the livelihood investigation will be the foundation for development, prioritizing and observing. There is though, no single arrangement or approach for livelihood investigations, nor has DFID established specific methods for such scrutiny. The emphasis is on using the best of available methods for the given conditions. There is, on the other hand, a distinctive DFID sustainable livelihood framework (Fig 3.1) that delivers an organizing arrangement for examination. The sustainable livelihood framework is fundamental to the Sustainable Livelihoods Approach.

The DFID framework works as follows:

1. A standing point in the recognition of how individuals work in a vulnerability context that is formed by diverse elements - unstable seasonal limitations (and prospects), monetary shocks and longer-term developments.
2. There is also a sensitivity to how people behave with diverse forms of livelihood capitals or assets in dissimilar arrangements which are shaped by: the vulnerability context, a variety of organizations and procedures and how they utilize their strength base to develop a variety of livelihoods approaches to accomplish their livelihood outcomes.

Figure 1: Department for International Development (DFID) Model

The major component of SLF is a framework that shows stakeholders as functioning in a Vulnerability Context, in which they access to particular assets. Assets gain weight and value through the principal social, institutional and administrative elements of the environment. This framework outlines the livelihood options that are open to people searching for their self-defined valuable livelihood aspirations and consequences (Kollmair & Gamper, 2002)

2.4.4 Capital and Assets

In DFID's framework, there are five kinds of capitals visualized as corners of a pentagon that is intended to highlight their interrelatedness. The five effects are also known as livelihood assets which are physical, human, financial, social and natural. These can too be referred to as social capital, human capital, financial capital, physical capital and so on. The terms "capital" and "asset" are unevenly substitutable in this framework, excepting that the term "capital" highlights the idea of possible depletion or investment. Every aspect might have admission to an exclusive set of these effects, though shapes of proprietorship/convenience might be very different in a given social setting.

The livelihood approach is grounded on the evidence that the asset position of the MSEs are vital to accepting the choices available to them, the approaches they accept to achieve livelihoods, the consequences they seek to, and the vulnerability context under which they work (Fraser, 2011). Correspondingly, it points out that people's assets are not only of value to an economic livelihood, but they also give sense to an individual's life. Capital or assets are both the means individuals utilize in structuring livelihoods, and such assets that offer individual capabilities "to be and to act". Moreover, the right to access and use the assets could be argued to be the most imperative element of all in terms of structuring sustainable livelihoods (Elliott, 2012).

Every capital is essential though obviously the degree of their significance will vary from household to household and over the period of time. Without a doubt, societies might substitute a number of capitals for others if they consider it more suitable for livelihoods, and that exchanging might reverse at some other time (Bebbington, 1999).

2.4.5 Vulnerability Context

Once these capitals have been identified and assessed for the contribution they make (or could make) it is necessary to explore the vulnerability context in which they exist; what are the trends (over time and space), shocks and stresses? The Vulnerability Context refers to the external environment in which people are living. For instance, national and international economies, trends in population growth, politics and technology, natural resources, diseases, economic shocks, prices, health or employment opportunities can also put a severe impact on livelihoods (Birkmann et al., 2013). Moreover, the vulnerability context denotes the trends, seasonality and shocks that impact people's livelihoods. The important quality of these features is that they are not easily regulated by households and/or the operators; however they do have some control in the medium or short term (Mach & Mastrandrea, 2014). Therefore, it is very vital to recognize ways by which the damaging effects of the Vulnerability Context can be diminished. This is may be through strengthening livelihood safety and building greater flexibility and diversity to the existing crises.

2.4.6 Micro and small enterprises and Sustainable livelihoods

Micro and small enterprises has been carefully chosen as a subject for study for the reason that it characterizes a feasible way out of poverty by giving improved and more specialized revenue streams for poor families. For instance, Micro and small enterprises activities have been witnessed to improve livelihoods by reducing vulnerability and risk, by establishing monetary and non-monetary resources, and by sponsoring economic and social liberation. Banchirigah et al. (2010) indicates that micro and small enterprises that are commercial, although they may be to lesser in number, can better play a role in supporting livelihoods, for the reason of their greater growth, profits, and work-creating probability. Poor families on the whole will probably step in and step out of micro and small enterprises depending upon the seasonal demand, nature of the activity, the accessibility of capitals, and other social and personal factors.

When defining the Micro and small enterprises in terms of sustainable livelihoods framework, "MSEs are small revenue making enterprises that are operated and managed by the proprietor, frequently with the aid of his or her peers. MSEs is a livelihood approach that, if sustainable and successful, can get the livelihood consequences of the Micro and small enterprises and their families" (Lawrence et al., 2006).

part of the country and with different ethnic background. The dwellers' of the sub city is engaged in diverse economic activities including formal, informal and non formal trading and small scale businesses; from which small trading, weaving, organized MSEs play a great role to support the livelihoods of the households of the Dwellers.

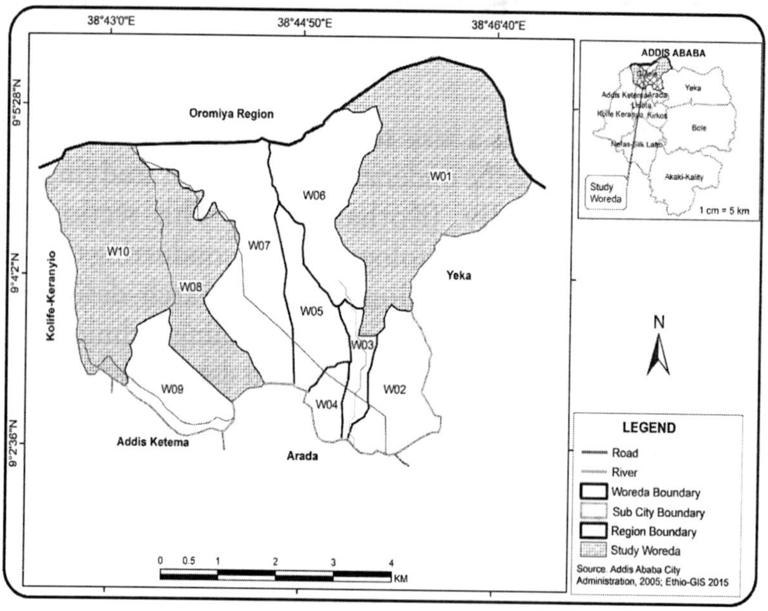

Figure 2: Source Addis Ababa City Administration 2005 Ethio GIS 2015

3.1.2 Gulele Sub City MSE Background

According to Gullele sub city micro and small enterprise office, growth oriented development and job creation clusters like manufacturing sector, construction sector, service sector, urban agriculture, and trade sector respectively creating job for youth and female about 27868,62836, 26967, 6940,and 6940 within the first GTP one (i.e., during the periods of 2003-2007 EC). Among this number 71% of employment are youth and 41% are female operators.

The MSE office report also outlined in the same period there are about 2540 enterprises were organized based on growth-oriented sectors. Besides, about 409,085,419 million birr loan was provided by Addis loan and saving association office to organized enterprises. On the other hand between 2003 to 2007 years, the enterprises also supported by providing a direct market linkage through undertaking different trade fair programs and exhibitions. The offices also found market assessment to create market linkage among and between SMEs, and among medium and large scale industries. By providing this market opportunity about 398,670,127 birr was gained by more than 12,161 enterprises.

Gullele sub city MSE office built and distributed 197 working sheds for the above main growth oriented sectors with in the year of 2002 to 2005. Above all, to modernize the production sectors the sub city was built 34 G+4 building for enterprises organized by Leather and textile, and trade sectors to offer them good working places and different shopping areas. For the success of the program especially the ground floors areas were given to the poor unemployed youth and women.

3.2 Design of the Study

As the main purpose of the study is to investigate the role of micro and small enterprises in realizing sustainable urban livelihood by considering Gulele sub city as case study; the study design will be descriptive survey with both quantitative and qualitative methods of analysis. Hence, Yin (2003) shown that, in situations where two strategies might be considered attractive, it is possible to use multiple strategies in a given study. The quantitative data will be gathered by using survey with semi structured questionnaire whereas the qualitative information will be collected by using in depth interview and document analysis methods.

3.3 Sources of Data

On the base of the study objectives, the researcher will be used both primary and secondary data sources. The secondary data sources will be collected from previous records to describe the general characteristics of the correlates of the effects of MSEs for sustainable urban livelihoods. Whereas the primary data sources will be gathered from the study population that includes MSE operators, experts and officials using structured and semi-structured questionnaires, including closed and open ended questions, which verify the objective of the research.

3.4 Sample Size and Sampling Techniques

Sample size may depend upon the nature of the population of interest or the data to be gathered and analyzed, and hence, subject availability and low cost factors are legitimate considerations in determining appropriate sample size (Best and Kahn 1999). To carry out the study and to meet the objective of the research, the researcher employed both probability and non-probability sampling techniques. To collect the quantitative data, multi-stage probability sampling methods will be used to select the samples from target MSEs included in this study, see Table 1 below.

Table 1: Target MSEs from which the sample taken

No.	*Selected MSEs District profiles*						
	District	*Manu.*	*Construction*	*Trade*	*service sector*	*Urban Agriculture*	*Total*
1.	1	140	100	291	13	6	550
2.	8	131	68	207	8	11	425
3.	10	63	69	2	29	18	181
	Grand Total						1156

Accordingly, the sample size for collecting quantitative data for this research is determined by using (Cochran's, 1977) formula by adding 10% contingency rate to enhance sampling representativeness. Therefore, the study used the following formula to calculate sample size.

$$n = \frac{N}{1 + N(e^2)} + 10\%\ \text{Contingency rate}$$

Where: n = the sample size the research uses; N= total number of MSEs operators in the selected study areas; e= maximum variability or margin of error 5% (.05); 1= the probability of the event occurring.

Therefore:

$$n = \left(\frac{1156}{1} + 1156(0.0025)\right) + 10\% = 297.17 + 29.72 = 326.9 \simeq 327$$

After calculating, the sample size one of the basic steps required in a given study is how to address fair distribution of sample across the target groups and their management process. As a result, initially, the districts in the sub-city will be stratified since they have separate administration boundaries to use as the base for sub grouping of samples. Hence, followed by random (using lottery method) selection of three Districts; namely, District 1, 8, and 10. Moreover, to select sample MSE operators from the mentioned districts random selection using lottery method will be applied. Accordingly, from each of the selected districts representative samples of operators will be drawn using their production areas and clusters; and followed by calculation of probability proportional to their size (Figure 2).

Moreover, from non-probability sampling methods purposive sampling approach will be applied to select respondents who have direct relationship with the study issue and who can show interest to share their experience and understandings; which addressed by in-depth interview guide. Accordingly, 3 selected Key MSE Operators (one from each district), 5 employees (i.e., one from each districts' and two

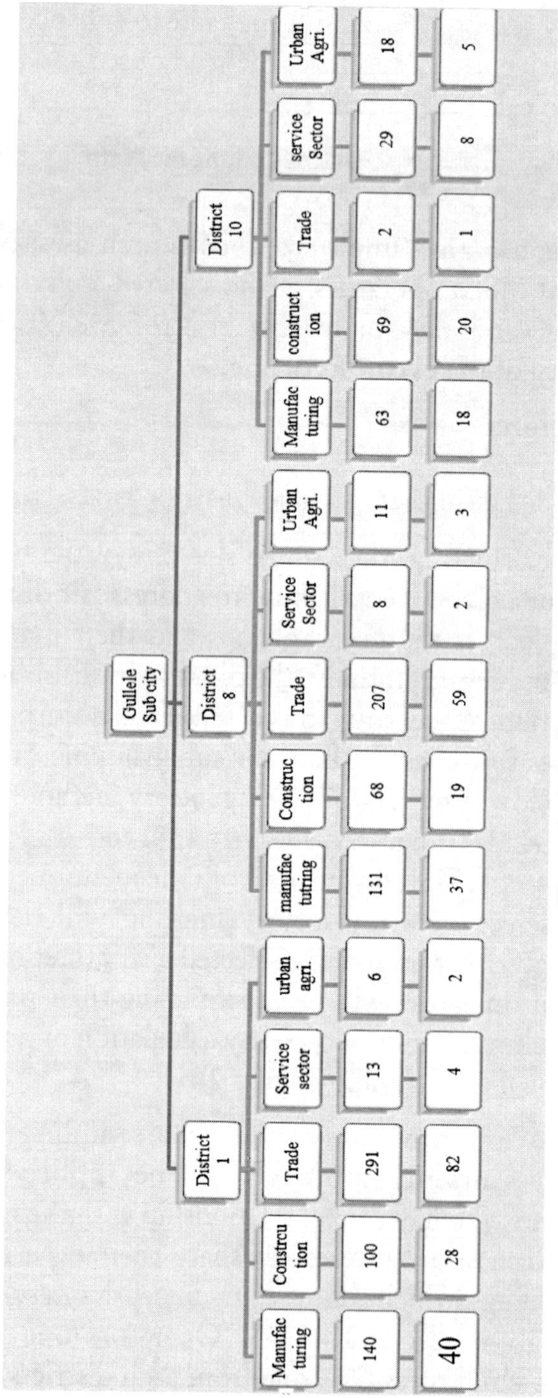

Figure 2: Sample Design for Analysis

from the sub city), and 5 government officials leading the sector (i.e., one from each district and two from the sub city officials be selected to include in the in-depth interviews. In sum, the study will consider 327 survey respondents (the operators, since they are the main focus of the study) and 13 major stakeholders work for the success of MSE program achievement (i.e., the major stakeholders will be addressed by purposive sampling).

3.5 Data Collection Instruments

The instruments employed to gather the necessary data for this study will be questionnaire, in depth interview, and document analysis. According to Cohen and Manion, (1994), use of combination of methods is suggested as having advantages to correct some of the deficiencies of any one source of data. Therefore, the data gathering processes considers the above mentioned instruments.

3.5.1 Questionnaire

Questionnaire is one of the instruments developed based on the reviewed literatures to collect relevant and reliable information from the respondent's to answer the basic question raised. Questionnaire is a cost effective, simple and quick way to collect quantitative data. One additional benefit of the questionnaire is the privacy that it affords to its subjects/respondents. For the reason, livelihood questionnaire developed by the researcher will be used to collect the quantitative data. Hopefully, the adapted questionnaires in English language guided the researcher (i.e., by assuming no language barriers for collecting important data) and contribute a lot for data collected from the respondents.

3.5.2 InDepth Interview

In-depth interview is a qualitative data collection method,

which offers to capture rich, descriptive data about the people's behaviors, attitude and perceptions, and unfolding complex processes. It can be used as a single method and/or as part of the multi method design approach like in the current study basing their importance. In depth interview is a loosely structured interview. And it allows freedom for both the interviewer and the interviewee to explore additional points and change direction. Thus, semi-structured interview guide will be prepared to collect the qualitative data. Therefore, representative of MSEs operators, experts, and officials who have more experience about the issue and truly discussed the existing reality will be involved in the face to face interview and addressed by interview guide. Consequently, the researcher interviewed each participant up to 50-60 minutes for each at one time. Recording will be also made based on the consent agreement before interview.

3.5.3 Document Analysis

Another option for data collection used in the study is document and record review, which is important in pertaining to the issue of data triangulation. Documents and records give the researcher access to the necessary background information and insights into the research problems. Thus, previous studies, policy documents, bulletins, journals, published or unpublished documents, magazines etc. will be used as important sources for the study.

3.6 Data Collection Procedures

First, permission will be asked from the Gullele sub city and selected districts administrations. Following, four assistant data collectors will be employed; who had previous experience in data collection and trained for one day on the content of the questionnaire and interviewing techniques. Instruction for data collectors will be given in order to obtain the consent of respondents before they administer the questionnaire, explain the objective of the study and ensure the respondents that data collected from them is confidential and used only for academic purposes. The filled and returned questionnaires will be revisited and edited for their completeness.

3.7 Method of Data Analysis

Data collected from the survey will be entered into a computer for analysis mainly using micro soft Excel and Statistical Package for Social Sciences (SPSS). Before running the analysis, some internal consistency checks will be made to assess the quality of data. The analysis part consists of descriptive statistics including frequency and cross tabs; and inferential statistics like t test, correlation, multivariate factor analysis, and regression analysis. Moreover, the data will be collected through open-ended questionnaire and in-depth interviews analyzed and narrated following the quantitative data results and/or described separately in areas of needs.

3.8 Validity and Reliability

3.8.1 Validity

According to Leedy and others (2005), validity is the ability of an instrument used to measure what it is designed to measure. The major issues required while assessing and confirming validity about the determination of adequacy of sample size, the needs of the use of different data collection tools, alleviation of the problem arises from Hartshorne effect, and to generalize the findings research to other similar setting; required examining content validity, internal validity and external validity.

3.8.1.1 Content validity

Content validity achieved when the study covered by adequate sample size by employing appropriate sample size determination techniques. The instrument developed and/ or adopted from previous study should require being exhaustive enough to answer the study raised (Leedy and others, 2005). Accordingly, the survey questionnaire adopted by the researcher for the investigation of the role of MSEs for sustainable urban livelihoods will be modified and addressed with some question to make it more adequate and representative of the problem raised. In addition, Leedy and others (2005) suggested the use of multiple sources of evidence, establishing chain evidence and having key informants reviewing draft of the study report. Grant (2008) also advised the use of the instrument especially survey questioner with the support of different data collection appropriate for the field in order to match the establishment of a competitive positioning. Thus for the current study in addition of survey questionnaire the researcher will be employed in-depth interview guide and content analysis data collection instruments.

3.8.1.2 Internal validity

Internal validity refers to whether the effects observed in the study are because of the treatment of the explaining factors/independent variables and not some other factors. Meaning, there is causal relationship between the dependent and independent variables (Cronbach and Meehl, 1955). This can be improved by controlling extraneous variables, using standardized residual, counter balancing, and by eliminating demand characteristics and investigator effects. Moreover, to overcome the adverse effects of Hartshorne responses, the respondents will be well informed with the covering letter about the ethical issues such as confidentiality of the information they provide, and brief description of research objectives.

3.8.1.3 External validity

External validity refers to the extent to which the results of the study can be generalized to other settings (ecological validity), other people (population validity), and overtime (historical validity) (Cronbach and Meehl, 1955). In other words, how the conclusions drawn can be generalized to other contexts (Leedy et al., 2005). External validity can be improved by setting experiments in a more natural setting and using random sampling to select participants.

3.8.2 Reliability

According to Cameron (2007), reliability is a measure of the extent to which the result of the research can be repeated with the same result if the research is replicated. Furthermore, Cameron et al (2007) states that in order to increase reliability, the researcher should use the same template as far as possible and use static methods in nominating the scale of the survey questionnaire. Accordingly, Cronbach's alpha test will be run to measure the internal consistency and the reliability of the questionnaire. As a result, the alpha coefficients for the overall survey questionnaire of investigating the role of MSEs for sustainable urban livelihoods will be made. Meaning, according to Mueller (1986) the Cronbach's alpha test value for overall survey questionnaire to be workable and researchable must have value of greater or equal to 0.5, and hence, in this study the assumption will be made by Muller and other scholars.

3.9 Ethical considerations

The respondents included into this study will be consulted after obtaining their prior informed consent. As the objective of the research is to examine the role of MSEs for sustainable urban livelihoods, initially respondents will be informed that the data collected from them only be used for academic purpose. Maximum efforts will be made to give full freedom of termination or continuations of the respondents while undertaking the data collection processes. In general, nothing has been done without the knowledge of the respondents.

Chapter Four

Summary of Findings and Discussions

4.1 Instrument Completion Rate

This part of the study presents about the completion and return rate of the instruments of the role of micro and small enterprises for sustainable urban livelihood survey questionnaire which was adapted by the researcher. By giving proper attention and selecting another respondent for those who did not show interest of participation the researcher tried to cover all the needed sample size though there were few non response rates for some parts of the questionnaire.

4.2 Socio Demographic Profiles of the Operators

The socio-demographic profile of the respondents includes gender, age, marital status, educational status, year of establishment, and family size of the operators. Accordingly, 289 (88.4%) males and 38 (11.6%) females were participated in the study. The result had shown the presence of statistical difference among gender in participating in MSEs at the study site (i.e., supported by the *Chi-Square value of* 10.632; $p < 0.05$). The other Socio-demographic factory is age of the respondent which is one of the basic demographic variables especially in determining performance achievements, emotional and skill development of the MSEs. In this view,

Table 4: Socio Demographic Profiles of the Operators

Socio Demographic indicators			*MSEs sector*					*Total*	*Chi-Square Tests*	
			Manufacturing	*Construction*	*service*	*Trade*	*Urban agriculture*		*Value*	*Sig.*
Sex	Male	Count	76	58	14	131	10	289	10.632[a]	.031
		%	26.3%	20.1%	4.8%	45.3%	3.5%	100.0%		
	Female	Count	18	9	0	11	0	38		
		%	47.4%	23.7%	0.0%	28.9%	0.0%	100.0%		
Total		Count	94	67	14	142	10	327		
		%	28.7%	20.5%	4.3%	43.4%	3.1%	100.0%		
age categorized	< =30 years	Count	51	36	10	49	8	154	25.064[a]	.002
		%	33.1%	23.4%	6.5%	31.8%	5.2%	100.0%		
	31-40 years	Count	28	18	0	50	0	96		
		%	29.2%	18.8%	0.0%	52.1%	0.0%	100.0%		
	> =41 years	Count	15	13	4	43	2	77		
		%	19.5%	16.9%	5.2%	55.8%	2.6%	100.0%		
Total		Count	94	67	14	142	10	327		
		%	28.7%	20.5%	4.3%	43.4%	3.1%	100.0%		
Marital status	Married	Count	62	43	9	113	5	232	10.186[a]	.037
		%	26.7%	18.5%	3.9%	48.7%	2.2%	100.0%		
	Single	Count	32	24	5	29	5	95		
		%	33.7%	25.3%	5.3%	30.5%	5.3%	100.0%		
Total		Count	94	67	14	142	10	327		
		%	28.7%	20.5%	4.3%	43.4%	3.1%	100.0%		

(Contd...)

4.3.1.2 Saving

Saving is one of the most important activities for the enterprises to expand their businesses and accumulate wealth's. Accordingly the data collected from the MSEs shown the presence of significant difference in accumulating wealth and household's capital. For instance, before organizing into MSEs nearly half of the respondents were not have the experiences of saving. But they are organizing into the MSEs the operators have significantly grown their experiences of saving. As a result, about 88.4% of the respondents have saving experiences (Table 6).

Table 6: Table comparisons of saving practices before and after organization into MSEs

Response category			*Do you have saving before organizing into MSEs in Banks/MFI?*		*Total*
			Yes	*No*	
Do you have saving AFTER organizing into MSEs in Banks/MFI?	Yes	Count	19	155	174
		% of Total	5.8%	47.4%	53.2%
	No	Count	19	134	153
		% of Total	5.8%	41.0%	46.8%
Total		Count	38	289	327
		% of Total	11.6%	88.4%	100.0%

Chi-Square Tests

Tests	*Value*	*df*	*Asymptotic Significance (2-sided)*	*Exact Sig. (2-sided)*	*Exact Sig. (1-sided)*
Pearson Chi-Square	7.283[c]	1	.007		
Continuity Correction	5.180	1	.023		
Likelihood Ratio	9.576	1	.002		
Fisher's Exact Test				.009	.009
Linear-by-Linear Association	7.206	1	.007		
N of Valid Cases	327				

Source: Field survey 2019.

4.3.2 Human Asset/capital

In the current study the human asset/capital represents upgrading their education, getting Entrepreneurship and BDS training, experiencing skill development and technology adaptation that help to pursue different livelihood strategies and achieve their livelihood objectives.

4.3.2.1 Upgrading Educational status

Upgrading educational statuses of the respondents were the main determinant factor for the livelihood security and eradication of poverty. Since human capital appears to be the general framework for the livelihood asset, and/or a building block of achieving livelihood outcomes. Many people considers lack of education as core dimensions of poverty and thus overcoming these conditions may be one of their primary livelihood objectives (DFID, 1999). Accordingly, the analysis of the current study verified

Table 7: Upgrade of formal education after organizing into MSEs

MSEs			*Upgrade of formal education after organizing into MSEs*		*Total*
			Yes	*No*	
MSEs sector	Manufacturing	Count	76	18	94
		% of Total	23.2%	5.5%	28.7%
	Construction	Count	37	30	67
		% of Total	11.3%	9.2%	20.5%
	Service	Count	0	14	14
		% of Total	0.0%	4.3%	4.3%
	Trade	Count	81	61	142
		% of Total	24.8%	18.7%	43.4%
	Urban agriculture	Count	0	10	10
		% of Total	0.0%	3.1%	3.1%
Total		Count	194	133	327
		% of Total	59.3%	40.7%	100.0%

Chi-Square Tests

	Value	*df*	*Asymptotic Significance (2-sided)*
Pearson Chi-Square	53.829[a]	4	.000
Likelihood Ratio	63.881	4	.000
Linear-by-Linear Association	19.262	1	.000
N of Valid Cases	327		

a. 1 cells (10.0%) have expected count less than 5. The minimum expected count is 4.07.

Source: Field survey 2019.

the educational attainments progress of the selected MSEs after organizing into MSE's were shown the presence of remarkable progress as compared with before organizing into enterprises. This confirms the contribution of organizing into the different sectors of the MSEs have tremendous effect in improving the livelihoods of the operators. As a result, *Pearson Chi-Square* test had shown the absence of statistically significant educational status improvement among the MSEs at $P = 0.000$ (Table 7).

4.3.2.2 Entrepreneurship and BDS training

Obtaining entrepreneurship and BDS training have paramount importance for the development of the micro and small enterprises. Because having the knowledge of Entrepreneurship may grow the success opportunities of the operators. As a result the data displayed in table 8 below shown good progress for delivering entrepreneurship knowledge and the skill of Business development trainings. Hence, on the average the study area delivered entrepreneurship and BDs trainings for about 76.5% of the MSE operators.

Table 8: Obtaining entrepreneurship and BDS training

MSEs Response Category			*Entrepreneurship and BDS training*		*Total*
			Yes	*No*	
MSEs sector	Manufacturing	Count	81	13	94
		% of Total	24.8%	4.0%	28.7%
	Construction	Count	40	27	67
		% of Total	12.2%	8.3%	20.5%
	service	Count	2	12	14
		% of Total	0.6%	3.7%	4.3%
	Trade	Count	125	17	142
		% of Total	38.2%	5.2%	43.4%
	Urban agriculture	Count	2	8	10
		% of Total	0.6%	2.4%	3.1%
Total		Count	250	77	327
		% of Total	76.5%	23.5%	100.0%

(Contd...)

Chi-Square Tests			
	Value	*df*	*Asymptotic Significance (2-sided)*
Pearson Chi-Square	73.700[a]	4	.000
Likelihood Ratio	65.526	4	.000
Linear-by-Linear Association	.033	1	.855
N of Valid Cases	327		
a. 2 cells (20.0%) have expected count less than 5. The minimum expected count is 2.35.			

Source: Field survey 2019.

4.3.2.3 Experiencing Skill Development and Technology Adaptation

Formal education is certainly not the only source of knowledge-based human capital as it also considers both the informal and non formal education for positive growth of their livelihoods. Hence, it is equally important to understand the ways of skill Development and Technology Adaptation; how this is shared, added to and what purpose it serves. As a

Table 9: Experiencing Skill Development and Technology Adaptation

MSEs response category			***Experiencing Skill Development and Technology Adaptation***		***Total***
			Yes	***No***	
MSEs sector	Manufacturing	Count	66	28	94
		% of Total	20.2%	8.6%	28.7%
	Construction	Count	40	27	67
		% of Total	12.2%	8.3%	20.5%
	service	Count	5	9	14
		% of Total	1.5%	2.8%	4.3%
	Trade	Count	116	26	142
		% of Total	35.5%	8.0%	43.4%
	Urban agriculture	Count	3	7	10
		% of Total	0.9%	2.1%	3.1%
Total		Count	230	97	327
		% of Total	70.3%	29.7%	100.0%

Chi-Square Tests			
	Value	*Df*	*Asymptotic Significance (2-sided)*
Pearson Chi-Square	28.247[a]	4	.000
Likelihood Ratio	27.111	4	.000
Linear-by-Linear Association	1.896	1	.168
N of Valid Cases	327		
a. 2 cells (20.0%) have expected count less than 5. The minimum expected count is 2.97.			

Source: Field survey 2019.

reason, some of these skills and technology adaptation may be gained from Technical and vocational trainings colleges and technology transfer and adaptations institutions; which able to enhance the MSE's capability to produce in modern ways, increase efficiency and effectiveness.

Accordingly, the current study had shown about 70.3% of the participants have high Experiences of Skill Development and Technology Adaptation exercises (Table 9) though there are statistically significant difference among MSE sectors at $P < 0.01$.

4.3.3 Social capital

Social capital is among the dominant prerequisite for sustainable management of urban livelihoods (Pretty, 2003). In the context of the current study social capital is taken into consideration whether the MSE's improved their social status and networking's or not. The analysis result had shown the presence of statistically significant improvement in the social status of the respondent's. As a result, bout 76.5% of the MSE operators had confirmed as their social status and networking's with other social groups are increased significantly at $P < 0.01$ (Table 10).

Table 10: Social capital comparison before and after organizing into MSEs

			Do have good social status and networking'sbefore organizing into MSE's		*Total*
			Yes	*No*	
Do have good social status and networking's after organizing into MSE's	Yes	Count	58	212	270
		% of Total	17.7%	64.8%	82.6%
	No	Count	19	38	57
		% of Total	5.8%	11.6%	17.4%
Total		Count	77	250	327
		% of Total	23.5%	76.5%	100.0%

(Contd...)

Chi-Square Tests					
	Value	*Df*	*Asymptotic Significance (2-sided)*	*Exact Sig. (2-sided)*	*Exact Sig. (1-sided)*
Pearson Chi-Square	3.672[a]	1	.055		
Continuity Correction[b]	3.043	1	.081		
Likelihood Ratio	3.451	1	.063		
Fisher's Exact Test				.023	.013
Linear-by-Linear Association	3.661	1	.056		
N of Valid Cases	327				
a. 0 cells (0.0%) have expected count less than 5. The minimum expected count is 13.42.					
b. Computed only for a 2x2 table					

Source: Field survey 2019.

4.3.4 Physical Capital

Physical capital in accordance of sustainable livelihood framework refers to existence of physical requirements like basic infrastructure needed to support the livelihoods of the local community (Lax and Krug, 2013). It includes productive assets that can be used as tools for production and household equipments (Sherbinin *et al.* 2008). Hence, the comparisons made before and after organizing into MSEs were shown as there are statistically significant differences on the capability physical asset per households. Accordingly, about 88.4% of the MSEs confirmed as there are significant improvements in endowment of basic household equipments and production materials extent after organization into MSEs (Table 11).

4.3.5 Natural capital

One of the basic factors in determining urban livelihood is access to housing and shelter for the households. Accordingly, the data collected from the field had shown as the respondents included in this study had shown remarkable progress in having their own private houses and/or having shelter through renting. For instance, among the MSEs included in this study about 79.8% those who are not have access to personal either through renting and creating privately, have

Table 11: comparison of basic household equipment and production materials before and after organizing into MSEs

Response categorized			*Basic households and production materials extent before organization into MSEs*		*Total*
			Yes	*No*	
Basic household and production materials extent after organization into MSEs	Yes	Count	38	230	268
		% of Total	11.6%	70.3%	82.0%
	No	Count	0	59	59
		% of Total	0.0%	18.0%	18.0%
Total		Count	38	289	327
		% of Total	11.6%	88.4%	100.0%

Chi-Square Tests

	Value	*df*	*Asymptotic Significance (2-sided)*	*Exact Sig. (2-sided)*	*Exact Sig. (1-sided)*
Pearson Chi-Square	9.466[a]	1	.002		
Continuity Correction[b]	8.135	1	.004		
Likelihood Ratio	16.187	1	.000		
Fisher's Exact Test				.000	.000
Linear-by-Linear Association	9.437	1	.002		
N of Valid Cases	327				

a. 0 cells (0.0%) have expected count less than 5. The minimum expected count is 6.86.

b. Computed only for a 2x2 table

Source: Field survey 2019.

Table 12: comparison of whether the MSEs have personal rent and/or private house before and after organizing into MSEs

Response categorized			*Do you you're your personal rent and/or private house before organizing into MSEs?*		*Total*
			Yes	*No*	
Do you you're your personal rent and/or private house after organizing into MSEs?	Yes	Count	54	215	269
		% of Total	16.6%	66.0%	82.5%
	No	Count	12	45	57
		% of Total	3.7%	13.8%	17.5%
Total		Count	66	260	326
		% of Total	20.2%	79.8%	100.0%

Chi-Square Tests

	Value	*df*	*Asymptotic Significance (2-sided)*	*Exact Sig. (2-sided)*	*Exact Sig. (1-sided)*
Pearson Chi-Square	3.702[a]	1	.062		
Continuity Correction[b]	3.03	1	.011		
Likelihood Ratio	3.51	1	.033		
Fisher's Exact Test				.021	.023
Linear-by-Linear Association	3.661	1	.045		
N of Valid Cases	327				

a. 0 cells (0.0%) have expected count less than 5. The minimum expected count is 13.42.

b. Computed only for a 2x2 table

Source: Field survey 2019.

changed their status and capability to have house either trough renting and/or creating privately (Table 12).

4.4 Determinants of MSEs household's wellbeing/ wealth status

4.4.1 Households livelihood wellbeing

As a result of its difficultness to analyze household livelihood wellbeing/ wealth through direct use of each of the household asset characteristics collected from the field survey data, it required variable standardization before running the investigations. Hence, one way to summarize the different asset of household characteristics across the different sectors of the MSEs is through adapting the principal component of variable analysis (PCA). The PCA can measure those variables having different characteristics, i.e., categorical with Likert scale and/or continuous variables, by changing into transformed standardized coefficients of the variables. For instance, five scale likert from strongly disagree to strongly agree (i.e. ranges 1-5) was used by Cope et al (1986), and quoted in Beaumont (2012). Moreover, the PCA also offers solution for change in having one given asset is stronger indicator of relative wealth and the assumptions of each asset change during the study period contributes equally in measuring household livelihood wellbeing index, since it determines the relative importance of each variable to summarize a set of variables (DeVellis 2012).

Since, the main objective of application of PCA to create one summary measure of household livelihood wellbeing (Vyas & Kumaranayake 2006), it relies on different statistical assumptions. For instance, in survey data with different variables that have correlated in unknown ways, PCA can reduce such variables and their relationships to each other by creating a new set of variables called principal component.

The order of the variance of the principal component shown differences among the variables, for instance, the first principal component refers to the largest possible variance across the given variables. The first principal component accounts for the largest possible variance across the specified variables. Likely, each succeeding component accounts for as much of the remaining variance as possible and are not linearly correlated to any of the preceding variables.

Based on this first principal component, each variable is given a 'factor weight.' The factor weight represents the relative importance of each variable to the constitution of the first principal component. Once the PCA has been done, extraction of the factor weights for each variable is undergone through multiplying the standardized variable by the factor weight, and then adds all the values together to calculate household livelihood wellbeing index scores for each respondent of the study area. Then, after, by using the country's poverty index reported currently i.e., which is 22.7% (MOFED, 2018) quartile classification was made. The reason why the cut point for the classification of livelihood wellbeing index was based on the quartile rather than classifying into quintiles, which is the most usual approach of classifying livelihood wellbeing indexes, is to consider the relatively poor operators adequately in the first quartile using the mentioned national reported data.

4.5 Determinants of MSEs household's wellbeing/ wealth status

To examine the effects of determining factors of MSEs on household livelihood wellbeing, the index cut point generated from principal component analysis was used to classify household into four quartile groups. For instance, those households having urban livelihood wellbeing of less than or equal to -.5290 cut point into the first quartile, .0071 for the second quartile, .5152 in the third quartile, and with cut point of less than or equal to 2.8405 in the fourth quartile. Meaning, as we go from quartile 1-4 the households calculated wellbeing value increases, showing the more accumulation of the assets. Thus, to find the effects of land use/cover changes on livelihoods of the urban community, it considers the mentioned households quartile wellbeing categories as a dependent categorical variable in multinomial logistic regression i.e., Q1= the 1st 25%, Q2 = the 2nd 25% or 50%, Q3= the 3rd 25% or 75%, and Q4 = the 4th 25% or 100%.

Moreover, the independent variables data collected through five scales Likert scale was recorded as dummy categorical variables, since the multinomial logistic regression result output organized for each independent variable with respect to each categorical dependent variable, which may complicates the understanding ability of the reader and data management techniques. Hence, the independent variables of financial problems, training adequacy problems, skill shortage, technology use and adaptation problems, inadequacy of production area facilities, in availability shopping and display area, attitudinal problems, and good governance problems were computed so as to examine their role on wellbeing of urban livelihoods at household levels. Accordingly, those independent variables shown statistically significant difference in explaining the dependent variables (i.e., wellbeing level) were selected after passing through the different assumptions of multinomial logistic regression analysis.

4.5.1 Regression analysis

To run regression analysis one has to stick on a number of different relevant assumptions to characterize the features and interrelation of the variables which includes analysis of Multi-collinearity effects and model characteristics.

4.5.1.1 Multi collinearity effects

Analysis of Multi-collinearity effects in the multinomial logistic regression detected by examining the standard errors for the B coefficients. A decision rule of a standard error larger than 2.0 indicates numerical problems and needs rejections of the variables. Hence, none of the independent variables in this analysis had a standard error larger than 2.0, confirm absence of Multi-collinearity effects.

4.5.1.2 Determining how well the model fits

The model summary table 13 provides information on the how well the model fits, which can be used to determine regression model-fits the data. The initial log likelihood value (411.815) is a measure of a model without considering the independent variables, but only a constant or intercept. The final log likelihood value (293.501) is the measure computed after all of the independent variables have been entered into the logistic regression. The difference between these two measures is the model chi-square value (118.314 = 411.815 - 293.501) that is tested for statistical significance. This test similar with *F*- test in linear regression of R^2; which tests whether or not the improvement in the model associated with the additional variables is statistically significant. Hence, in the current study, the model *Chi-Square value* of 118.314 is significant at $p < 0.01$, which confirm the presence of statistically significant relationship between the dependent and independent variables included in the model.

Table 13: Model summary of multinomial logistic regression

Model Fitting Information				
Model	*Model Fitting Criteria*	*Likelihood Ratio Tests*		
	-2 Log Likelihood	*Chi-Square*	*Df*	*Sig.*
Intercept Only	411.815	118.314	24	.000
	293.501			

The next step in multinomial logistic regression output is checking the strength of the relationship between the dependent variable and the independent variables, and also referrers to the proportion of variance in the dependent variable that can be explained by the independent variables. Accordingly, there are three ways of explaining such variance in logistic regression analysis i.e., Cox and Snell, Nagelkerke, and McFadden R^2 measures. That is, the higher R^2 measure indicates, the greater model fit. For instance, both the R^2 value of .529 and .551 stated in the model summery table 14 shows the independent variables explain 52.9% and 55.1% of the variability of the dependent variable, livelihood wellbeing.

Table 14: Proportion of variance

Pseudo R-Square	
Cox and Snell	.529
Nagelkerke	.551
McFadden	.344

Moreover, the Chi-Square (Table 15) tests whether the overall regression model is a good fit for the data and/or checks whether the model as a whole is significant. In other words, it confirms the adequacy of the independent variables, taken together, in predicting the dependent variable better than just predicting the mean scores. The table 15shows that the independent variables statistically significantly predict the dependent variable, Chi-Square $= 175.568$, $p < .05$ (i.e., the regression model is a good fit of the data).

Table 15: Best fit model

Goodness-of-Fit			
Chi-Square		Df	Sig.
Pearson	175.568	150	.105
Deviance	166.032	150	.175

four households. The households found in the quartile 2 also to reduce by 32.2%. In quartile 3 the probability of the households' wealth accumulation was to reduce by 42.5% as compared to Quartile 4 households due to Training adequacy problems and quality.

Skill Shortage

The multinomial logistic regression confirm necessary skill shortage create statistically significant difference on households wellbeing at $p < 0.05$ in quartile 1. As a result, the households' wealth accumulation more likely to reduce by 64.4% from Quartile 4 MSEs households, if assumed other things are remains constant. In the same way, MSEs households in quartile 3 were also affected by skill shortage and hence their livelihood wellbeing was more likely to reduce by 61.5%.

Technology use and adaptation problems

In the same way, technology use and adaptation problems, is also more likely to decrease the status of the MSEs households livelihood wellbeing/wealth accumulation by 91.2% in the 1st quartile, 89.9% in the 2nd quartile, and 73.7% in 3rd quartile as compared to households in the 4th quartile. The severity of the impact was increases with decrease in livelihood wellbeing classes, i.e., the poorest and the relatively poor MSEs households are more vulnerable than those of medium and better off categories.

Inadequacy of the availability of shopping and display area

Inadequacy of the availability of shopping and display area shown statistically significant difference among the households of 2nd quartile, and hence it resulted in reduction of MSEs households livelihood wellbeing by 93.1% as compared to households in the 4th quartile.

4.6 Coping strategy by wealth classes

Livelihoods in many urban areas of the world are complex and dynamic; perhaps the one constant is the day-to-day uncertainty of survival (Marschke and Berkes, 2006). The concept of livelihood is about individuals, households, or groups making a living, attempting to meet their various consumption and economic necessities, coping with uncertainties, and responding to new opportunities (Haan and Zoomers, 2003). That is, MSEs who faced different challenges at current risk of work problems will develop strategies to minimize the challenges on their livelihoods. Accordingly, Finding Loan from families and relatives; Developing positive attitudes for MSEs and personal work(aiming for change); Getting business trainings by their own; Finding alternative production area including rent; Renting shopping and display area; Finding alternative market linkage and advertizing; and Finding and adapting technologies were the frequently used strategies to alleviate the challenges of the MSE sector, and ranked from 1 up to 6 basing their importance (Table 18).

Table 18: Coping Strategy used to minimize the challenges

Coping Strategy			*MSEs by Wealth classes*				*Total*	*Rank*	*Chi-Square Tests*	
			Q1	*Q2*	*Q3*	*Q4*			*Value*	*Sig.*
What strategy you and your family use to overcome the challenges of the MSE sector?	Finding Loan from families and relatives	no.	17	19	20	23	79	1st	*89.97*	*.000*
		%	20.7	23.2	24.4	28.0	96.3			
	Getting business trainings by their own	no.	9	12	13	11	45	3rd		
		%	11.0	14.6	15.9	13.4	54.9			
	Finding alternative market linkage and advertizing	no.	9	9	11	9	38	4th		
		%	11.0	11.0	13.4	11.0	46.3			
	Finding and adapting technologies	no.	7	7	8	11	33	6th		
		%	8.5	8.5	9.8	13.4	40.2			
	Finding alternative production area including rent	no.	14	9	8	7	38	4th		
		%	17.1	11.0	9.8	8.5	46.3			
	Renting shopping and display area	no.	9	11	7	9	36	5th		
		%	11.0	13.4	8.5	11.0	43.9			
	Developing positive attitudes for MSEs and personal work (aiming for change)	no.	17	15	15	12	59	2nd		
		%	20.7	18.3	18.3	14.6	72.0			
Total		No.	82	82	82	82	327/8			
		%	100	100	100	100	100			

Source: Field survey 2019.

Chapter Five

Conclusion and Recommendation

5.1 Conclusion

On the basis of the objective of the study and findings discussed the following conclusions have been made.

To examine the role of Micro and Small Enterprises for Sustainable Urban Livelihood the five asset/capitals that households endowed with were analyzed by comparing before and after organizing into MSEs. Moreover, to determine their effects on households' livelihoods, the mentioned basic capitals/assets were aggregated and summarized using principal component analysis.

Accordingly, the findings of the study revealed, as average net income of MSEs were increased by 2474.359 birr/month after organizing into the different sectors of the MSEs; and hence significantly grown their saving experiences. The educational status, skill development and technological transfer adaptation capabilities of the selected MSEs after organizing into enterprises were also shown remarkable progress as compared with before organizing into enterprises.

The social capital taken into consideration whether the MSE's improved their social status and networking's or not; had shown the presence of statistically significant improvement in their social status. The comparisons made before and after organizing into MSEs were also shown the

References

A. Berihu , Z. Abebaw and T. Biruk (2014). "Identifying key success Factors and Constraints in Ethiopia's MSE Development: An Exploratory Research Report 14," Ethiopian Development Research Institute, Addis Ababa.

Abor, J., & Quartey, P. (2010). Issues in SME development in Ghana and South Africa. International Research Journal of Finance and Economics, 39(6), 215-228.

Abraham, D. (2003). "Local Economic Development (LED) in South Africa: A useful tool for sustainable development", Urban Forum Vol. 14, pp. 185-200

Adato, M., & Meinzen-Dick, R. (2002).Assessing the impact of agricultural research on poverty using the sustainable livelihoods framework. Washington: IFPRI.

Advani, A. (1997). Industrial clusters: A support system for small and medium sized enterprises: Private Sector Development Department, World Bank.

Ageba, G. and W. Amha (2004). Policy Impact on Regulatory Challenges of the Micro and Small Enterprises (MSE) in Ethiopia. Second International Conference on the Ethiopian Economy.

Agyapong, D. (2010). Micro, small and medium enterprises' activities, income level and poverty reduction in Ghana–A synthesis of related literature. International Journal of Business and Management, 5(12), 196-205.

Amare Abawa (2017). Micro, Small and Medium Enterprises (MSMEs) Development Strategies in Ethiopia: Retrospective and Prospective Analysis. IRACST – International Journal of Commerce, Business and Management (IJCBM), ISSN: 2319–2828 Vol. 6, No.1 Jan-Feb 2017 11. Online available: www.iracst.org/ijcbm/papers/vol6no12017/3vol6no1.pdf.

Amha, W. and Ageba G. (2006). Business development services (BDS) in Ethiopia: Status, prospects and challenges in the micro and small enterprise sector. International Journal of Emerging Markets, 1(4), 305-328.

Ardic, O. P., Mylenko, N., & Saltane, V. (2011). Small and medium enterprises: a cross-country analysis with a new data set. World Bank Policy Research Working Paper Series, Vol. 5538.

B. Thorsten , D.K. Asli and L. Ross , (2005). "SMEs, Growth, and Poverty: Cross Country Evidence," The World Bank, Washington DC.

Banchirigah, S. M., & Hilson, G. (2010). De-agrarianization, re-agrarianization and local economic development: Re-orientating livelihoods in African artisanal mining communities. Policy Sciences, 43(2), 157-180.

Bebbington, A. (1999). Capitals and capabilities: a framework for analyzing peasant viability, rural livelihoods and poverty. World development, 27(12), 2021-2044.

Bekele, E. and Muchie M. (2009). Promoting micro, small and medium enterprises (MSMEs) for sustainable rural livelihood. DIIPER & Department of History, International and Social Studies, Aalborg University.

Bennett, N. J., & Dearden, P. (2014). Why local people do not support conservation: community perceptions of marine protected area livelihood impacts, governance and management in Thailand. Marine Policy, 44, 107-116.

Berhanu, E. (2005). Role of micro and small enterprises in local economic development: The case of Awassa. Local economic development in Africa: Enterprises, communities and local development, 96-123.

Berihu, A., Abebaw, Z. and Biruk, T. (2014) *Identifying key success factors and constraints in Ethiopia's MSE development*: an exploratory research, Ethiopian Development Research Institute, Addis Ababa.

Best and Kahn (1999); **Research in Education**: seventh edition: prentice-Hall of India: New Delhi.

Birkmann et al. (2013). Framing vulnerability, risk and societal responses: the MOVE framework. Natural hazards, 67(2), 193-211.

Birkmann, J. (2006). Measuring vulnerability to promote disaster-resilient societies: Conceptual frameworks and definitions. Measuring vulnerability to natural hazards: Towards disaster resilient societies, 1, 9-54.

Bowale, K. & Akinlo, A. (2012), 'Determinants of Small and Medium Scale Enterprise Performance and Poverty Alleviation in Developing Countries: Evidence from South West Nigeria', European Journal of Humanities and Social Sciences, Volume 17, Number 1, pp. 846 863. ISSN 2220-9425.

Cameron, L, SL Wise, and SM Lottridge. (2007). The Development and Validation of the Information Literacy Test. *College and research libraries* 68 (3):229.

Carney, D. (2003). Sustainable livelihoods approaches: progress and possibilities for change. London: Department for International Development.

Chambers R. and Conway G. (1992). *Sustainable Rural Livelihoods: Practical concepts for the 21st Century.* IDS Discussion Paper 296, IDS, Brighton, UK.

Chambers, R. (1987). Sustainable livelihoods, environment and development: putting poor rural people first.

Chambers, R. (1992). Sustainable livelihood thinking: an approach to poverty, environment and development.

Cochran, W. G. (1977). Sampling techniques (3rd ed.). New York: John Wiley & Sons.

Cohen, L., & Manion, L. (1994). **Research Methods in Education** (4th ed.). London: Routledge Publishers.

Cohen, L., & Manion, L. (1994). **Research Methods in Education** (4th ed.). London: Routledge Publishers.

Coulthard, S. et al. (2011). Poverty, sustainability and human wellbeing: a social wellbeing approach to the global fisheries crisis. Global Environmental Change, 21(2), 453-463.

Cowen, Michael P. and Shenton, Robert W. 1995 'The Invention of Development', in J. Crush (ed.) *Power of Development*, London: Routledge, 27-43

Cronbach, L. J., & Meehl, P. E. (1955). Construct Validity in Psychological Tests. Psychological Bulletin, 52, 281-302.

Dent, D., Dubois, O., & Dalal-Clayton, B. (2013). Rural planning in developing countries: supporting natural resource management and sustainable livelihoods. Routledge.

DFID (Department for International Development). (1999). Sustainable Livelihoods Guidance Sheets. London. Accessed on December 21, 2018 from http:// www.livelihoods.org/info/info guidancesheets.html

Elliott, J. (2012). An introduction to sustainable development. Routledge.

Fabayo, J. A. (2009). *Small and Medium Enterprises development strategy: A critical Option for sustainable Long–Term Economic Development in Nigeria.* Paper presented at the first Annual International Conference on: Effective Management of Small and Medium scale Enterprises for sustainable Economic Development held at Abraham Adesanya Polytechnic, Ijebu-Ode held from25-27 August.

FDRE Ministry of Trade and Industry, (1997). "Micro and Small Enterprises Development Strategy," Addis Ababa.

Ferrol-Schulte, D., Wolff, M., Ferse, S., & Glaser, M. (2013). Sustainable Livelihoods Approach in tropical coastal and marine social–ecological systems: A review. Marine policy, 42, 253-258.

Fraser, E. D., et al. (2011). Assessing vulnerability to climate change in dryland livelihood systems: conceptual challenges and interdisciplinary solutions. Ecology and Society, 16(3), 3.

G. Tom and V. Van der , "Defining SMEs: a less Imperfect Way of Defining Small and medium Enterprises in Developing Countries," 2008. [Online]. Available: www.brookings.edu/ ~ /media /research/files/ papers/2008/9/development% 20gibson/09_development_gibson.pdf.. [Accessed 03 january 2019].

Garoma, B. F. (2012). Determinants of Microenterprise Success in the Urban Informal Sector of Addis Ababa: A Multidimensional Analysis, International Institute of Social Studies of Erasmus University (ISS).

Gebrehiwot, A and wolday, A. (2004). *Micro and small enterprise development in Ethiopia Survey Report. Addis Ababa*

Gebremeskel H. Gebremariam1 Tesfa G. Gebremedhin, and Randall W. Jackson (2004). THE Role of Small Business In Economic Growth And Poverty Alleviation In West Virginia: An Empirical Analysis Research Paper 2004-10.

Geleta, D. S. (2013). Socio-economic Contributions of Micro and Small Enterprises: The Case of Jimma City. Science, Technology and Arts Research Journal, 2(2), 123-134.

Hisrich, R., et al. (2009). Entrepreneurship. Second Canadian Edition: McGraw-Hill Ryerson (ISBN 978-0-07-097984-0).

Independent Evaluation Group (IEG), (2013). "Approach Paper Evaluation of the World Bank Group's Targeted Support for Small and Medium Enterprises," IEG World Bank, Washington DC.

Iorio, M., & Corsale, A. (2010).Rural tourism and livelihood strategies in Romania. Journal of Rural Studies, 26(2), 152-162.

Kabir, Hou, Rahima, Wang & Wang (2012). Impact of small entrepreneurship on sustainable livelihood assets of rural poor women in Bangladesh. International Journal of Economics and Finance, 4(3), 265.

Kollmair, M., & Gamper, S. (2002). The sustainable livelihoods approach. Input Paper for the Integrated Training Course of NCCR North-South Aeschiried, 9-20.

Kongolo, M. (2010). Job creation versus job shedding and the role of SMEs in economic development. African Journal of Business Management, 4(11), 2288-2295.

Kongolo, M. (2010). Job creation versus job shedding and the role of SMEs in economic development. African Journal of Business Management, 4(11), 2288-2295.

Kothari, CR. (2004) Research Methodology Method and Technique. (2nd Ed). New Delhi, New Age international publisher.

Lawrence, S. R., et al. (2006). Sustainability practices of SMEs: the case of NZ. Business strategy and the environment, 15(4), 242-257.

Leedy, P.D., & Ormrod, J. E. (2005). **Practical research: Planning and design** (8th ed.). Upper Saddle River, NJ: Prentice Hall.

Lukács, E. (2005). The economic role of SMEs in world economy, especially in Europe. European Integration Studies, 1 (4), 3-12.

Mach, K., & Mastrandrea, M. (2014). Climate change 2014: impacts, adaptation, and vulnerability (Vol. 1). Cambridge, New York, NY: Cambridge University Press.

Ministry of Trade and Industry (1997). *Micro and Small Enterprises Development Strategy.* Addis Ababa Ethiopia.

Mukras, M. (2003). Poverty reduction through strengthening small and medium enterprises.

Mulu Gebreeyesus (2007). Growth of Micro-Enterprises. Empirical Evidence from Ethiopia Development Research Institute.

Naudé, W., & Krugell, W. (2002). African Economic Growth: Wrong to Rely on Small Businesses?*. Journal of Small Business & Entrepreneurship, 16(2), 21-44.

Nichter, S., & Goldmark, L. (2005). Understanding micro and small enterprise growth. Micro Report(36).

Olomi, D. (2006). Policy dialogue seminar paper on opportunities and challenges for rural SMEs development in Tanzania. Economic and Social Research Foundation (ESRF)

Peci, F., Kutllovci, E., Tmava, Q., & Shala, V. (2012). Small and medium enterprises facing institutional barriers in Kosovo. International Journal of Marketing Studies, 4(1), p. 95.

Phaho, D., & Pouris, A. (2008). From Silos to Synergies: An Institutional Framework for the Growth & Sustanability of Innovative SMEs in South Africa. Paper presented at the ICSB World Conference Proceedings.

Sallu, S. M., Twyman, C., & Stringer, L. C. (2010). Resilient or vulnerable livelihoods? Assessing livelihood dynamics and trajectories in rural Botswana. Ecology and Society: a journal of integrative science for resilience and sustainability, 15(4).

Schmitz, H. (1995). Collective efficiency: Growth path for small-scale industry. The journal of development studies, 31(4), 529-566.

Scoones, I. (2009). Livelihoods perspectives and rural development. The Journal of Peasant Studies, 36(1), 171-196.

Small, O. (2004). Medium-sized enterprises in Turkey: issues and policies: Paris: OECD.

Sokoto, A. A., & Abdullahi, Y. Z. (2013). Strengthening Small and Medium Enterprises (SMEs) as a Strategy for poverty Reduction in North Western Nigeria. American Journal of Humanities and Social Sciences, 1(3), 189-201.

Soltani, A. et al. (2012). Poverty, sustainability, and household livelihood strategies in Zagros, Iran Ecological Economics, 79, 60-70.

Stephen M. (2013). A Critique of Theory and Practice. Springer Dordrecht Heidelberg.

Vyas, S and Kumaranayake, L (2006). Constructing social-economic status indices, How to use PCA. Health Policy and Planning 21, 6, 459-468.

Williams, W. (2006). Supporting the growth of small and medium enterprises. Address to the Nova Committee of the Trinidad and Tobago Chamber of Industry and Commerce.

Winfred Jr, A. (2006). Pro-poor Economic Growth: Role of Small and Medium Sized Enterprises. Journal of Asian Economics, 35-40.37.

World Bank Group, (2015). "4th Ethiopia Economic Update: Overcoming Constraints in the Manufacturing Sector," World Bank group, Washington DC.

Yin, R.K (2003). Case Study Research Design and Methods (3rd ed.)London: Sage publications.

Abbrevations

BM	:	Bottom- Micro
CSA	:	Central Statistics Agency
DFIDs	:	Department for International Development
FeMSEDA	:	Federal Micro and Small Enterprises Development Agency
GDP	:	Gross Domestic Product
IEG WB	:	Independent Evaluation Group World Bank
IJCBM	:	International Journal of Commerce, Business and Management
MFI	:	Micro Finance Institutions
MM	:	Middle Micro
MSEs	:	Micro and Small Enterprises
NGOs	:	Non Governmental Organizations
OECD	:	Organization for Economic Cooperation and Development
SLA	:	Sustainable Livelihood Approaches
SLF	:	Sustainable Livelihoods Framework
TM	:	Top Micro
UNIDO	:	United Nations Industry and Development Organization

Index